I0170892

Unlock Your Hamster Workbook

Volume One of
The Sit 'N' Do Nothing
Hamster Series

Humans All Make Some Time Exploring Relationships

Written by Wendy Proteau

Covers designed by Wendy A Proteau

Introduction

There are many professionals, doctors and celebrities who have advice about how we should live. It seems everyone has an opinion, except the individual. There are many great books available, but we tend to find their own way by stubbornly following our programming. We've lived differently than the experts and do what we feel is best. Ask yourself how many times you've given advice to friends or family only to watch them do their own thing.

Life comes at us daily. We make hundreds of decisions a day like what to do, what's for dinner, what's on my schedule etc… We all live thinking tomorrow will always come and no matter what happens, that hamster of ours keeps running on the wheel in our minds. We go through many things in this life. Life's twists and turns force us to ask, what do I do now? In a perfect world we'd all live exactly as we want, but the truth is that life is never easy and it puts us to the test every day. We spend time in our own heads thinking about the present, past and future. While shopping, driving, cooking or out with friends…that darn hamster just keeps going because life doesn't stop. When the tough moments come, it derails.

How do I know? My family was thrown one hell of a curve ball when dad, our hero, was diagnosed with terminal cancer. Being told he had two weeks to four months was a bombshell. The next heart wrenching months nothing else mattered but time with him. It was then that I realized there was so much I didn't know. What did he think of life? What did he feel his best achievements were? Did life turn out as he dreamed? What was his favorite memory? I forgot to ask so many things while growing up thinking we had time. He was only 68 years old and I never did get the chance.

Over four hundred people came to pay tribute and I wondered if he knew how many people cared for him in his lifetime. Did he realize how loved he was? Did he know he had touched that many lives? Had they told him how they felt? Did I tell him enough before I lost him? Look around in your world and ask yourself the same, because sometimes we miss that opportunity.

Later that year I learned of a friend who needed a surgery that would slow him down. I went to the store to find things to keep his brain busy and there were crosswords, books, magazines, but I decided to put his hamster to work. I wanted to create something to help him through. That's where this all started by reaching out to someone I care for. I wanted to never forget to ask the questions of everyone in my life.

I thought about the millions who face everyday challenges. Why is it we only stop and reflect when something goes wrong? We put off until tomorrow, then when it comes we ask, why did I wait? That doesn't make sense. So I continued the series and my humor kicked in. We are all an accumulation of every moment we've gone through from birth until now. It formed every aspect of who we are, just as we've shaped people around us. Why not create a fun way to connect with people in the here and now.

It seems in this day and age we're so busy with work, bills, kids, schedules, technology…I believe we're missing out on something important…taking the time to just share moments with friends, family and reaching out to new acquaintances. Why not learn about our differences and try to understand each other more? We are all boneheads at times. We've all made mistakes. We are individuals with so much in common. We grow, learn, love, foible, fail, succeed, make mistakes, hurt, care…we really are all the same when you stop to think about it.

When is the last time you talked to a stranger at a bus stop, grocery store or in a waiting room? When's the last time you slowed down to get to know someone in your hectic day or took a moment to show kindness to a stranger? Friends used to take the time to make that coffee date. With emails and texts, we keep in touch via technology. Can you really share who you are in a text? Pretty hard to text a life altering situation or defining moment, isn't it? Would you email a private experience or memory? Are we losing human contact?

There are so many people reaching over the internet, but delete has become the new 'easy button.' It's teaching that rejection is a click away. Even cell phones have an ignore button, so are we really bridging the distance or are we being trained to stop opening up, afraid of being judged?

Face it, the bills will always come, obligations and schedules will always be there, but if we slow down we just might not miss out on the most important thing-who we are and those around us.

This series covers different situations, even curious thoughts about the world. From old to young we all think about life. We are the sum total of what we've done, thought, learned and experienced up until this very moment. We have opinions, dreams and preferences, so let's start laughing together again.

This could be a self-check about your life or something to work on with the people in your life. Whether friends, family, your buddy, neighbor, coworker, or single person you've had your eye on…what better way to open communication than handing them something that asks who they are inside and out? Discuss thoughts, memories, goals, or leave it on the coffee table for people to read. In this fast-paced world of computers this may seem like a foreign idea. Why not bring us a little closer? There are several editions…I tell ya this hamster never stops!

GOTTA BE HONEST!"

"Unlock your Hamster"

Little known facts about: _____ and what I think!
First Name please

Today's date:_____

This will get us warmed up for the rest of the book. It also gives us a chance to look back years from now at who we are in this moment. Ok, so let's start with the basics of who you are on paper, shall we?

My last name is: _____

I live in: _____

I was born: _____ day_____ month _____year

I was born in: _____
(City please)

Time I was born: _____ am/pm

I was raised in _____

But other cities/towns I've lived over the years:

_____

_____

_____

_____

_____

My education level is: _____

The Sit N Do Nothing Hamster Series

I went to the following schools
(Names and years please)

_____

_____

_____

_____

I work as a _____

I have been at my current job _____years/months

In 3 words, I would describe myself as:

1_____

2_____

3_____

This book was given to me by: _____

In 3 words, I would describe the person who gave me this book as:

1_____

2_____

3_____

See, not so hard is it? Kick back, relax and let's start our journey!

UNLOCK YOUR HAMSTER

Volume One

1-These just a yes or no answer. There are no maybes, close or only once options. If you've done it (even if you never got caught) gotta say yes! Everyone has done some crazy things in this lifetime…have you ever?

Felt road rage	_____yes	_____no
Stolen something	_____yes	_____no
Held a grudge too long	_____ yes	_____no
Got into a fist fight	_____yes	_____no
Lied to a friend	_____yes	_____no
Cheated or thought about it	_____yes	_____no
Broken a heart	_____yes	_____no
Lost your temper	_____yes	_____no
Played a bad joke	_____yes	_____no
Not paid a debt	_____yes	_____no
Lied to the boss	_____yes	_____no
Played hooky	_____yes	_____no

2-Well maybe you haven't done many of the above, so on a scale from 1-10, where 1 is living an upstanding lifestyle and 10 meaning oops crossed too many lines:

I think overall, I am a: _____

If you received this book as a gift, the person who gave this to you in your opinion would be:

_____ (same scale 1-10)

3- Seems the world is busy and we're always on the go, so let's dream for a little bit. If you could right at this very moment do anything, where would you?

Dream vacation: _____

Like to be right now: _____

Like to see just once: _____
                         (Wonder of the world maybe?)

Like to retire: _____

4-Everyone's life is different and we work towards goals. At the back of your mind are the little dreams you wish for. I'd like to have a little ranch with horses on the edge of the mountains somewhere. Ah, if only. Whether we end up there or not, it's still something we hold onto. Now some people are content right where they are and never think of moving. If you could choose a place to be 10 years from now, ideally you would:

Stay where you are   _____yes _____no

Move to another province/state/country   _____yes _____no

Which city & country:_____

Own a country place/cabin   _____yes _____no

Move closer to where you grew up   _____ yes _____no

Live near mountains   _____ yes _____no

Have a hobby ranch   _____ yes _____no

Live on a tropical island   _____ yes _____ no

Live near a beach   _____ yes _____no

What is your dream:

_____

_____

5- People accumulate toys in life....motorcycles, trucks, horses, cars, electronics, sports equipment, games, etc...

What 3 toys do you still want to add to the list? Now be realistic.

_____   _____   _____

6-You get up, go to work, come home and deal with normal everyday life, but are there things you still would like to try given the opportunity? These just answer a yes or no. You can add one you've always wanted to try:

Hot air balloon ride   _____

Sky Dive   _____

Drive a racecar   _____

Scuba dive   _____

Bungee jump   _____

Cliff dive   _____

Mountain climb   _____

I always wanted to _____

7-We all get into routines of everyday, but some things are just more fun or easier doing it with a significant other. I look forward to so much if I ever find Mr. Right. Some of you have found that person so you know the things you value most. Between 1-10-(10 being gosh darn wonderful) rate how you view each of these with a partner. If single, what do you think you would enjoy sharing with someone:

Getting advice   _____

Cooking dinner   _____

Going for a drive   _____

Grocery shopping   _____

Going to sporting events   _____

Entertaining people   _____

Watching a movie   _____

Going dancing   _____

Cold winter nights   _____

Someone to come home to   _____

Emotionally leaning on   _____ (yikes that's a tough one)

Someone challenging you   _____

Work around the house/yard   _____

Playing sports   _____

8-Here's an easy one, the basic things in life, what do you like best? Here you can only choose one or the other on each line (you can't check them both.) No deep thinking here, just the first thought that comes to mind. You prefer the following:
(Remember only check one off in each line)

Apple_____   Orange_____

Beef_____   Pork_____

Ice cream_____   Cake_____

Vanilla_____   Chocolate_____

Being on time_____   Running late _____

Dress clothes_____   Casual _____

Blondes_____   Brunettes_____   Redheads_____

Moon_____   Sun_____

Television_____   Music_____

Runners_____   Boots_____

Flip flops_____   Dress shoes_____

Pizza _____   Cheeseburger_____

Chips_____   Pretzels_____

Chinese food _____   Mexican food _____

Slippers _____   Barefoot_____

Dining out_____   Home-cooked_____

9-With computer technology we have the opportunity of meeting new people through work, game sites, date sites and chat rooms. I've met several people through the computer and have even taken the time to meet them in person. If you got to choose one person to meet how would you fanagle it all? What city would you arrange to meet in? It could be a contact through work or a casual friend you chat to. If you could plan it all:

I'd like to meet with them in: _____

What's the first name of the person you want to meet the most?

_____

Why would you like to meet them?

_____

What character traits do you like best about them?

_____

What's the first question you'd ask face to face?

_____

Are there others on your list you'd like to meet? Let's write a few names of those you'd like to finally shake their hand or hug. Put them in order of priority:

1 _____ 2 _____ 3 _____

If single, perhaps there is one in particular that you've sparked romantically with? Name please:

_____

10-This is to question things that people may not really know about you. It's all about favorites! You've probably never even thought about them all, but you do have them. So here we go, fill in your favorite for each category:

Color: _____   Pastime: _____

Movie: _____   Book: _____

Song: _____   Food: _____

Restaurant: _____   Place to be: _____

Game: _____   Sport: _____

TV show: _____   Underwear type: _____

Hero: _____   Cartoon: _____

Comic book: _____   Animal: _____

Wild animal: _____   City: _____

Vacation spot: _____   Color Shirt: _____

Thing to do: _____   Dessert: _____

Snack: _____   Drink: _____

Soda: _____   Lucky number _____

Vacation spot_____   Vehicle _____

What's your favorite saying:_____

. A lot of these are simple things that I never knew about my Dad and wish I'd taken the time to ask them. They are just little things, but I still wonder about them now that he's gone.

11-Profound sayings, some we believe in and some we don't. They can be comforting at times and at other times we say them as the only explanation that makes any sense for how things happen. Do you believe in any of these? Check off only the one's you truly believe in:

_____everything happens for a reason

_____a watched kettle never boils

_____what doesn't kill you, makes you stronger

_____when god closes a door, he opens a window

_____opposites attract

_____people get what they deserve (karma)

_____laughter is the best medicine

_____you can lead a horse to water…but you can't make him drink

Add your favorite: _____

12- Life is a mixture of trouble, boring, routine and happy moments. It's not like we all get up every day experiencing moments of utter joy (well I don't anyways), but we've had them. Thinking back to those moments filled with laughter and complete contentment, who was with you for the top 5 and how old were you at the time?

Name of person: Age:

_____   _____

_____   _____

_____   _____

_____   _____

_____   _____

13-Things that make you say what the? You see things that make you stop and question what were they doing or thinking. For example, when driving, I'll see one shoe in the middle of the road and ask myself, 'was the person walking and it slipped off? Did they just keep going? Did they not notice?' I put a few examples of the strange things I've witnessed and wonder if it's universal. Let's see if it happens all over the world.

a- Things on the road that just don't make sense (1 shoe on the road)

_____

_____

b- Nature doing something totally out of the norm- (a bird chasing a cat and the cat was running away!)

_____

_____

c- Kindness for no particular reason-(a friend handing out blankets to the homeless)

_____

_____

d-Someone throwing a fit and they're alone (A man yelling the top of his lungs in the grocery store at nobody…kinda scared me really)

_____

_____

e- Signs that just don't make sense to anyone (A no entry traffic sign at the end of a dead end street. Wow, who put that there, where would we go?)

_____

_____

f-Someone dancing in a public place but there's no music (That's usually me when I'm out with the nephews just to embarrass them. If you see us, dance with me, it'll embarrass them more!)

_____

_____

14- I've often thought I was born in the wrong century and believe I'm more in tune with things way back (A strange connection to the old west or days of knights and castles). I picture a simpler life. My friend's laugh saying I probably would've been a saloon gal or a serving wench (great friends, huh?). Do you feel a draw to a certain period? If you could go back in time which period do you think you should have lived in?

Period/time_____

What would you be_____

What do you think your friends would think you'd be:

_____

Why did you choose this time period:

_____

_____

_____

15-Now along that same thinking: If time travel was possible and you were forced into a time machine and you could pick any one time to go to for one day, what would you like to see for just 24 hours? Think hard, it could be dinosaurs, caveman, biblical times, Roman Empire etc…or the future for that matter and the space age they say is coming. For me, definitely the wild west-cowboys, horses…yep would be a dream.

Time would be _____

List what you would like to experience in that era

1_____

2_____

3_____

4_____

5_____

16-People have big dreams in life and there are many things that may become possible with time. Right now, it's only a chosen few who may have done some of these. If you could do absolutely anything, if it were all really possible, number the list below in order of preference 1-8: (#1 being first on your list)

_____take a trip into space

_____climb to the top Everest

_____walk on the moon

_____explore the depths of the pyramids of Egypt

_____see the bottom of the sea in a submarine

_____take a ride in a fighter plane at the speed of sound

_____explore area 51 and all its secrets

_____drive rocket engine vehicles on the salt sands (parachute to stop)

Add something adventurous that, you've always dreamed of doing:

_____

17-Some people are risk takers and some do the safe stuff and never even wonder about it all. I watch TV shows and movies about real life survival and wonder, how did they make it? I question whether I'd have the stamina they had. Most were in the wrong moment at the wrong time. If you had to say how well you'd fare, number these in the order that you think you'd be able to deal with.

#1 being yep, you could handle it to #15 being nope, wouldn't make it. (1-15)

_____lost in the Amazon
_____lost in the jungles of Africa
_____be a survivor of a plane crash on a mountain
_____a survivor of a sinking in the middle of the ocean
_____be a front line soldier in one of the World Wars
_____be a Prisoner of War for months (POW)
_____be stranded at the South Pole (brrrrr)
_____lost in the desert
_____on a deserted island-(No Gilligan's Island crew isn't there)
_____in an underground mine collapse
_____top floor of a burning high rise (all them stairs and smoke)
_____hunted behind enemy lines
_____taken hostage in foreign country
_____passenger of a hijacking
_____jailed in a foreign country

18-This is a question I think about all the time. If world war III ever hits, they say it will be the end of life as we know it. Movies and books portray how the end could happen and the few who crawl out of it. It scares me what technology can possibly do one day. I often say if there was a nuclear war, I'd pull out my lawn chair and sit closest to ground zero, I don't think I'd make it through the tough road ahead. Survival would kick in I'm sure (not eating cockroaches though-no way!) I have many questions about how I'd handle it all, how to prepare and what to do. We all have survivor instinct they say, so what would you prepare or plan for? Let's say you're given two days warning, you've only got 48 hours and it's really going to happen.

What would be the first 10 things? Write them in order (priorities ya know). Think about it, you have family, extended family, homes and friends. Would you call people? How would you prepare? In order I would:

1-_____

2-_____

3-_____

4-_____

5-_____

6-_____

7-_____

8-_____

9-_____

10-_____

That sure is something to think about, I suck at planning a weekend never mind the next two years of survival.

19-We all have something we always wanted to do out of the normal social events we're used to. For me, it's always been to attend a formal ball (the fancy gown type) just to see how the ritzy people live. (I'd be such a misfit and probably trip on the darn dress, but to do it once, I tell ya!)
Is there any you'd like to try once? It can be anything; ride with a bike gang, be a high roller in Vegas, schmooze with royalty?

_____

Do you foresee any problems like I do about fitting in, or tripping?

_____

_____

20- If you could go back to one time in your life and re-experience something exactly as it was, not changing a single thing, it has to be exactly as it was:

How old were you: _____

What was the occasion: _____

Who was there with you: _____   _____   _____

_____   _____   _____

Why: _____

_____

_____

21-We all have friends in life and of course we know them well, but I'm sure we all have at least one thing we never really asked them. Just something we're curious about. If you could ask that one question and they had to tell you the absolute truth-who and what would you ask? (top 3 and it can be family or friends)

Name   Question

_____   _____

_____   _____

_____   _____

While you're thinking about that list, if there was a question you could ask your higher power (whatever that may be), what would be the question?

_____

22-Ever look at your friends or family and ask yourself, "What were you thinking or why'd you go and do that?" Have you ever wanted to tell them any of the following: (Don't put the name, just think of the people that you've wanted to say it to and fill in the gaps.)

With the way you wear your hair, you look like a: _____

The way you dress reminds me of a: _____

You kinda smell of: _____

Your cologne/perfume smells like: _____

Your make-up makes you look:_____

You may think your all that but:_____

I love the way you: _____

I hate the way you: _____

23-Throughout life we meet people we kinda take a shine to. Maybe we're shy or it wasn't an appropriate time, but we had romantic thoughts (we just never said them out loud). Think about that person in your mind, could be past or present. (No names-so you're safe!) Fill in the rest of the sentence.

I have always wanted to take you

_____

I would love to get stranded with you for a month and

_____

If I could have you all to myself for a weekend, I'd want to

_____

I'd like to watch you play _____, just once.

I picture you often wearing _____

I wish I would hear you say_____

Your so cute when you_____

I think you have the cutest _____

24-Thinking about crushes, think back to your childhood, did you have a favorite babysitter?

Person: _____

How old were you at the time: _____

25-If you could check on one of your old flames, be a fly on the wall just see how their life is now (they wouldn't know you were checking on them), who would it be and why?

Who: _____

Why:

_____

_____

26-Ok, if you got this to keep entertained while in hospital the following will be clear as a bell. Perhaps you have to dig into your memory for a past experience. If you're in hospital or ever have been it's not so fun, is it? You have many nurses, attendants and doctors. Some you like…some, not so much:

Which shift is your favorite nurse on? _____am _____pm

Which shift is your favorite doctor on? _____am _____pm

Not so favorite nurse? _____am _____pm

Not so favorite doctor? _____am _____pm

Do you like your sponge bath person? _____yes _____no

27-If you've ever shared a room in hospital there are other patients in there with you. Sometimes you have great ones, sometimes not. I know I kept this poor lady awake all night and I'm sure she would've poked me in the eye if she could reach. So anonymous is always great, let's ask these questions:

Would ya have one moved if ya could? _____yes _____no

Do you enjoy the company? _____yes _____no

Are they talking too much? _____yes _____no

Do they snore? _____yes _____no

Do they pass wind a lot? _____yes _____no

Would you send them flowers if you could? _____yes _____no

Have ya taken a shine to them? _____yes _____no

Do they have noisy visitors all the time? _____yes _____no

Are they helping you along? _____yes _____no

28-Now the dreaded personal questions of being in hospital. We know what it's like, so here's the list to decide how you feel about your stay (or) if you ever stayed in one:

Bed feels like sleeping on _____

The bedpan feels like _____

I hear so many sounds, but _____makes me crazy.

The food tastes like _____

But so far my favorite is _____

It's not the greatest place to be, but I like _____

I really don't mind these gowns but I wish they'd

_____

_____

For me, those darn gowns just felt like they were too tight in some places and not tight enough in others. I really didn't like having the back open.

29- Movies, they create a world we can escape to for a while and you've probably seen a few that you wish you could really live out. If I could, I'd pick a love story or chick flick. Yep, that romantic perfect love scene would be nice! So if you could pick one movie to actually experience:

Which movie: _____

You'd want to be which character: _____

Why that movie:

_____

_____

Do you think you resemble any famous person?

I look like _____

Your friends would say_____

30-Here's a favorite, the world of cartoons! For those who know me, my hero is that smart mouthed rabbit who was always one up on everyone. If you could be any cartoon character in the world?

Who would you be: _____
Why:

_____

_____

Which cartoon do you most resemble now _____

Your friends would say_____ (gotta love friends huh?)

31-We all have favorite songs in life. Whether a theme to a movie or a song by a favorite band. When we hear it we naturally sing along. Which songs are they for you? Top 5 please:

1_____

2_____

3_____

4_____

5_____

Do you sing while driving?   _____yes _____no

Ever been caught and feel foolish?   _____yes _____no

Do you just keep on singing anyways? _____yes _____no

Do you sing in the shower?   _____yes _____no

Scale from 1-10 your singing ability is a: _____

Your friends would say: _____

32-Ah…life's embarrassing moments. Being caught doing something when we thought we could get away with it. Now this may sound like question #1, but these are actually when you're caught. Think back and ask yourself, have I been caught? (Just check em off…and be honest!)

In a lie: ____yes _____no

Playing hooky: _____yes _____no

Doing something illegal: _____yes _____no

Naked at the wrong moment: _____yes _____no

Farting and someone hears it: _____yes _____no

Or smells it (automatic guilt huh): _____yes _____no

Or worse it really was someone else you get blamed: _____yes _____no

Public fall, when ya hope nobody saw and you get up quick: _____ yes _____no

Doing something to look cool and it just turned out oh so wrong: _____yes _____no

Adjusting in the elevator and wow the doors open to an audience: _____yes _____no

You try to scratch that itch inconspicuously and poof someone comes around the corner: _____yes _____no

Completely unprepared for a meeting: _____yes _____no

Grumbling stomach at the quietest moments-like church or court: _____yes _____no

Having sex and someone walks in: _____yes _____no

Dropping food on the floor and scooping it up like it never happened and someone catches you: _____yes _____no

Singing with others to the song and the music stops and there you are: _____yes _____no

Did they all laugh? _____yes _____no

Walking in on someone in the stall using public restrooms: _____yes _____no

Walk in the wrong restroom not clearly reading the signs: _____yes _____no

Clothing tucked in the wrong places so you exposed yourself walking through a room: _____yes _____no

33-Ah, those fond memories, I bet you're snickering to yourself remembering them. Let's continue to those memories that make us smile. Do you remember all your firsts?

First crush was on _____

First crush on me was _____

First innocent kiss was from _____

First date was with _____

I was how old at that time _____

First real wow kiss was from _____

First real girlfriend/boyfriend _____

How long did it last _____?

First car I drove was a _____

First car I wrecked was a _____

First place I lived when I was on my own_____(street)

First base was with _____

First time I tried drinking I was _____

First time I had sex was with _____

I was how old _____

First time I fell in love I was _____years old

34-Well there's a lot of firsts when young and it usually gets better with time. Now we could go step by step, but let's dive right to the 'bests' so far in life. Looking back over your whole history:

Best vehicle I ever owned was a _____

Best memory was with _____

Best kiss of all time I got from_____

Best date of all time was with_____
We did:

_____

_____

Best boyfriend/girlfriend was_____

Why were they the best:

_____

_____

Best sex was with_____

Best thing I ever did was

_____

Best Performance in a sporting event was playing_____

What made it the best:

_____

Best Christmas present ever was_____

Best birthday was when I celebrated my _____

Why:

_____

35-Of course with the 'bests', come the opposite, 'the worst!'-Yikes! Here we go:

Worst punishment I ever got when I was a kid was_____

Worst date was with_____

Worst vehicle I ever had was a_____

Worst Christmas present I ever got was a _____

Worst kiss was from_____

Worst birthday was when I celebrated my_____
Why:

_____

Worst idea I ever had was _____

Worst pet I had was _____

Worst friend I ever had was_____

Worst movie I ever paid to go see was_____

Worst sex I had was with_____

Worst dinner cooked for me was by_____

We covered them all and I'm not saying you won't experience better or top the 'yikes' list, but isn't it fun to think back on those things. (Gotta take the good with the bad in life)

36- Now for personal grooming and how we present ourselves every day. We all have our habits. Some are high maintenance, some don't give a darn and I suppose everything in between. Let's ask a few questions-check what applies to you:

Do you think you're picky about your looks? _____yes _____no

What would your real friends say?: _____yes _____no

We shall see I suppose as you answer the following. Now some are meticulous and some are basic, so do you:

-Trim your nose hair? _____yes _____no

-Trim your ear hair? _____yes _____no

-Shape your eyebrows? _____yes _____no

      And if so, do you:

      Pluck _____Wax _____ Get em done professionally _____

-Ladies, how about your legs? How often do you remove hair?

Always: _____ When you feel like it: _____ Not at all: _____

If you do you either:

Shave: _____ Wax: _____ Sugar: _____ Professionally done: _____

-Now the Privates, do you?

Shave: _____ Wax: _____ Get professionally done: _____

-Do you manicure? _____ yes _____ no   How often____ per month

-Do you pedicure? _____ yes _____ no   How often____ per month

-If you could, what would you like to have done professionally all the time?

_____

-How many times do you?

Fix your hair in a day: _____

Brush your teeth in a day: _____

-Do you?

Use mouthwash: _____ yes _____ no

Do you floss: _____ yes _____ no

-How many times do you recheck the mirror before heading out? _____

-How many outfits do you try on when going out socially? _____

-Does it make your spouse crazy? _____ yes _____ no

Are they worse? _____ yes _____ no

-How many times do you go to the barber or salon in a year? _____

-How many times a week do you bathe or shower? _____

37-Everyone has habits, some good/some bad and some we never think twice about them. You see them in public and you wonder...why? Have you seen someone...

Spit in public: _____yes _____no

Belch loudly in public: _____yes _____no

Pick their nose: _____yes _____no

Does that hold the one nostril and blow out the other: _____yes _____no

Fart loudly in public: _____yes _____no

Scratch their privates: _____yes _____no

Walk around naked: _____yes _____no

Urinate in public: _____yes _____no

Yell in public places: _____yes _____no

Not all have the same manners that we do, they just have different standards. What is the thing that most disgusts you when you see it?

_____

38-We've all seen some icky stuff, so let's ask you the same questions. Just check off the ones you've done (even once), emergency or not!

Spit: _____

Belch: _____

Pick your nose: _____

Fart: _____

Scratch: _____

Public Nudity: _____

Urinate in Public: _____

Yell: _____

OK, enough of that stuff...ICK!

39-With all those makeover shows, I sometimes wonder what I'd look like with something new (a blonde perhaps). We're going to explore this. All these questions are if you could change just one thing about yourself for only 24 hours (just to try it out). But only one for each category-what would you change and why?

Hair: (you'd like to be a)

Blonde:_____   Brunette:_____   Redhead: _____

Other color: _____

Be bald: _____ or have hair: _____

Add length: _____ or shorter: _____

Why: _____

Your body is what it is right now, no wanting to make it younger, older or healthier...just work with what you got. Remember you're only changing one thing. It could be smaller waist, smaller chest, bigger chest, bigger arms, longer legs, shorter legs, muscular arms...etc. But only one thing for 24 hours-(it's a tough one)

I would like to have:

_____

Why: _____

_____

_____

39- We are all individuals and no two people are alike, kinda like snowflakes. So we learn to appreciate what we have. Now at times we are our own worst critics, but I'm sure there is one thing we like the best.

In your opinion, your best physical feature is:

_____

Your friends would say your best physical feature:_____

Your best characteristic or personality trait is:

_____

Your friends would say: _____

40- If you could change one physical thing on your best friend and partner (if applicable), what would it be and why?

Friends name: _____ Change:_____

Why:

_____

_____

_____

Partners name: _____ Change: _____

Why:

_____

_____

41-Enough about changing things, let's see what you'd do with the following: If you had to pick just one or the other and really do it (here again, only one on each line), like someone is paying you $5000.00 dollars just to watch you, would you:

Sing on stage: _____ or pole dance: _____

Bungee jump: _____ or skydive: _____

Water ski: _____ or snow ski down Whistler: _____

Climb a mountain: _____ or walk naked down a busy street: _____

Serenade someone in public: _____ or moon a crowded room: _____

Drive a stunt car: _____ or hi rise window cleaning: _____

42-How about pets, have any? They're the best! Always happy to see you and have time (they love unconditionally). They wait all day just to be with you. Do you:

Have one now _____yes _____no

What is/are they _____, _____, _____

Name(s) are/is _____, _____, _____

Best tricks_____

_____

_____

Would people say it looks like you _____yes _____no

How many pets have you had _____

What was your favorite one's name _____

Do you dress your pet/pets _____yes _____no

Does it mind _____yes _____no

I had pets while growing up starting with those crazy sea monkey things, remember those? Brine shrimp are no fun! We had several dogs, cats, rabbits and even 6 ducklings. The ducks were great when young, but as they grew up they chased and nipped at us. Mean ducks!

What was your first childhood pet's name _____

What type of animal _____

43-Since we're thinking of childhood, think back to old friends. Remember back when you were young and just starting to figure things out in life, those early teen years 13-16 when we still had lots to learn.

Who was your first teenage best friend _____

How long were you friends _____

Do you still keep in touch _____yes _____no

Favorite thing about them

_____

_____

Best memory was when you

_____

_____

_____

Worst fight was over

_____

_____

If you could see them again now, would you _____yes _____no

Now fast-forward to the here and now. Thinking of your life right at this very moment let's ask the same. We have both female and male friends (they make the world go round) so we'll cover both genders here:

Male friend:

Who is your best male friend _____

How did you meet

_____

_____

How long have you known them _____

How often you keep in touch _____

Favorite thing about them

_____

_____

Best memory so far

_____

_____

Worst fight so far was over

_____

_____

If you could pick a trip, anywhere in the world, to take with your best male friend right now, where would you go and why.

_____

_____

Female Friend:

Who is your best female friend? _____

How did you meet?

_____

_____

How long have you known them _____

How often you keep in touch _____

Favorite thing about them

_____

_____

Best memory so far

_____

_____

Worst fight so far was over

_____

_____

If you could pick a trip, anywhere in the world, to take with your best female friend right now, where would you go and why?

_____

_____

44-Everybody can usually do something unique that they don't tell a lot of people about. Call it a quirk, a hidden talent, something silly or something great. Whether it's being artistic or mechanically inclined, bending your body, putting your heel behind your head or even rolling your eyes in opposite directions:

Do you have any special talent _____yes _____no

What is it

_____

Have you shown anyone _____yes _____no

Will you _____yes _____no

45-Now for the romantic side of life-Woo Hoo! Yep, we all grow up and do crazy things sometimes. Things we look back on and say…gosh, what was I thinking? How'd we even manage that? Some call it live in the moment and some call it life experience. So let's delve into the sexy stuff. (See no names so you're safe)

Where was your first time _____

How old were you _____

How old were they _____

Scale from 1-10 on enjoyment level _____ (1 being woo hoo!)

Any regrets _____yes _____no

Do you wish you had waited _____yes____ no

If yes, till how old_____

Was your partner patient and understanding _____yes ____no

Were you in love at the time _____ yes _____ no _____thought so

We all live and learn, but at times crazy stuff happens in life, so let's see what you've gone through:

Where was the strangest place you ever had sex?

_____

Where was the most romantic?

_____

Where was the most uncomfortable place?

_____

Romance…that wonderful moment when the stars align, the moon is full and everything is going wonderfully. Ever notice they always have the perfect love scene in the movies? Ok, I must be doing something wrong!

If I could, I'd like to have that one night with that perfect partner. Soft music, candles, at a tropical island resort. Ok, I dream a lot, but if you could set up the perfect romantic night with that special someone, make all the plans, the ambience, mood-settings, let's see what you'd come up with:

Where would it take place

_____

What do you envision the place like

_____

_____

What mood settings would you have? (I gave you extra room, there are so many things you could choose-candles, rose petals, lace, leather…)

_____

_____

_____

_____

46-Since were onto sexy things, if you could spend one night with any famous person, actor/actress, singer, sports star, anyone at all-who would it be?

_____

We all had idols when we were young, so think back to those days, who were you absolutely in love with?

TV idol: _____

From what show_____

Movie star:_____

Favorite movie they were in: _____

Singer:_____

Favorite song _____

You sing along all the time _____yes _____no

Do you still know all the words _____yes _____no

Let's see if you can remember the song's first line:

_____

Which poster did you have on your bedroom wall _____

47-Growing up we had so many things we just loved to do. Let's think back to our earlier years, what were your favorites:

After school show: _____

Outside thing to do: _____

Inside thing to do: _____

Were you a good kid _____ yes _____ no _____ sort of

How often did you get in trouble _____ times a month

What was your favorite sport _____

What about a favorite board game _____

Who seemed to win most often _____

48-Did you play any of these group/friends games? Remember when you were all just hanging out after school and had nothing better to do?

Hop-scotch _____yes _____no

Hide n seek _____yes _____no

Peggy stick _____yes _____no

Kick the can _____ yes _____no

Dodge ball _____ yes _____no

7-up _____yes _____no

Spin the bottle _____yes _____no

Truth or dare _____yes _____no

Are we sparking some memories?

Your favorite was: _____

49-As we got older there were drinking games our friends introduced us to. Yikes! If mom only knew about these (just so you know Mom, it was my friends fault.) Did you play any of them? Do you remember any of these games- (clearly)?

Caps _____yes _____no

Jacks _____yes _____no

Bullshit _____yes _____no

Quarters _____yes _____no

What was your favorite _____

Did you win a lot _____(that you can remember)

Well I guess some of those games might have been a blur. They were fun way back when. As we get older, somehow we don't think of playing them anymore. Could be the 4 days it takes to recuperate. Responsibility takes over somehow, darn it!

50-With owing a house I wish I would have taken plumbing or electrical so I could tackle the repairs myself. Hindsight is always easy, huh? I'm sure for some it's to know how to paint, knit, draw or cook and for others it would be more challenging things. But life gets busy and we just never took the time to learn. Sitting where you are right now, if you could go back and learn more about just two things what would they be?

1-_____

2-_____

51-Some people keep learning all the time (It's never too late they say!) If you had the time and all your bills were paid, the obligations and stresses were gone,

Would you take a course _____yes _____no

What would it be _____

Are you taking a course now _____yes _____no

What is it _____

52-Growing up nowadays kids sure have a lot of fun toys and games. Wasn't like way back in the day of cards, checkers and the ever famous cardboard fridge box. Heck, we could play for hours with that darn box. Kids seem to have so much now.

Do you wish you could have had the games they have now _____yes _____no

Do you play any games now _____yes _____ no

What is your favorite _____

How many hours you spend gaming _____/hours per week

I often think kids today aren't as creative as we used to be. What do you think kids don't learn like you did, when you were young?

_____

_____

53-Seems things always move faster the older we get. If you look back from when you were young to now, people sure have a lot of things to make life easier and more convenient. But if you had to go back and live as your great-grandparents', grand parents' or parents' did, could you? Let's just see how well you do here.

Rate each line on a scale from 1-10 (1=you could handle it no problem and 10=there is no way I could do it)

_____Horse as transportation
_____Clotheslines-hang to dry everything
_____Hand washing (everything)
_____Hauling the water from the pump
_____Out houses
_____Collecting firewood for the winters
_____Cooking on wood stove
_____Canning/preserving all your own food
_____Making all your own clothing
_____Hunting for your food daily
_____Walking everywhere
_____Trapping
_____A barn Raising
_____Building everything with hand tools, no electricity
_____Raising 8 kids in a two/three room house
_____Milling your own flour for use
_____Churning butter
_____Horse and plow fields from sun up to sun down
_____Education was all aged kids in one lil room
_____Working from a young age on the family farm
_____Marry at a real young age
_____Arranged marriages
_____No heat except the fireplace
_____No lights only candles/lanterns
_____Beds made of straw

Ok, well that's way far back and kinda hard to imagine. Most of what we use has only been invented in this past 50 years really. Let's see how many conveniences you would be willing to do without. Think now, if we had to reduce energy due to crisis. Number from 1-24 (in order) the things you could do without- (1-being would miss it the most-24 being don't care if I lose it).

_____	Air conditioning
_____	Tub/whirlpool
_____	Cell phone
_____	Running water
_____	Heating
_____	Telephone
_____	Computer
_____	Dishwasher
_____	Microwave
_____	Toaster
_____	Oven or stove
_____	Vacuum
_____	Blenders/mixers
_____	Freezers
_____	Vehicle/cars
_____	Privacy (sharing bedroom with siblings)
_____	Food processors
_____	Lawnmower
_____	Electric lighting
_____	Bottled Cleaners
_____	Television
_____	Power tools
_____	BBQ
_____	Refrigerator

If you really think about it, we've got everything really rather convenient compared to way back, so you gotta wonder why is it we don't have more spare time? Things invented over the past century were created to make life easier and we certainly don't work like the settlers did from sun up till bed time, so why don't we have extra time?

54- I wonder what they'll come up with in the future. Already they're making robot people so you what's next? If you could ask them to invent just one thing to make your life easier (for me, it would be a clothes folder-I hate doing it…I keep waiting), what would you like to see them invent specifically for you?

_____

55-Now if you've ever been through a procedure, you're supposed to rest, relax and just heal. People who love you come around to visit. You know what it's like if you've ever been through a surgery. So in your past experiences or if you're going through something right now, let's ask:

How many people fuss over you _____

Who is/was the worst worrier _____

Who is/was the one who makes ya the most crazy _____

Who is/was helping you out the most _____

Who do/did ya wish was there most of the time _____

Who did ya wish would just leave ya be for a bit _____

Who have/did you snap at the most _____

(I know we love them for caring, but sheesh! Sometimes, we just get a bit moody when going through something.)

56-Hey! Let's change the subject. Ever wonder why we took some of those classes in school? I mean do you really need world history, geography or algebra for what you do in daily life? Maybe you do, but for me-not really. So if you could have designed school courses knowing what you know now, which courses didn't you need and what would you have replaced them with? Now these aren't real courses, for example-I didn't need that home economics course-should have taken the how to not get ripped off by mechanics course or how to fix a toilet course.

Didn't need: _____

Could have used _____

Didn't need: _____

Could have used _____

Didn't need: _____

Could have used _____

57-Do you remember your teachers from school? You went to school for a lot of years, some even went to University or College, so these would be over your entire school history:

Favorite teacher: _____
What grade were you in_____

You just hated sitting in this teacher's class: _____
What grade were you in_____

Teacher who was a bit off (shall we say): _____
What grade were you in_____

Teacher with the worst temper was: _____
What grade were you in_____

Teacher that most influenced you was: _____

Favorite physical education teacher: _____

Which teacher did you have a crush on _____

58-What was the best thing you learned while going to school? Now for some it was how to skip out and not get caught, while others social skills. Maybe it was the academics-Mathematics, English or Geometry.

_____

59- We all go to school and then begin finding our path in life. Hopefully, we meet a partner along the way, fall in love and build a life together. (Ok, well that doesn't always happen...I'm still looking!) So let's see where you are in life. I don't know if you're single or not, so this question is geared towards what you'd appreciate in the absolutely perfect partner. You may have found them or are still looking. What are the qualities you look for or have in a partner?

Now you won't be able to check these all…I don't think any one person has all these mixed up together. There are quite a few here to choose from, so think carefully and just check what applies to either your current partner or what you are looking for in your next.

_____ Strong family values	_____ Sexy
_____ Morals	_____ Risk taker
_____ Good kisser	_____ Older
_____ Younger	_____ Humor
_____ Kind	_____ Loves animals
_____ Loves kids	_____ Strong personality
_____ Intelligence	_____ Stubbornness
_____ Quiet type	_____ Independent
_____ Talkative	_____ Active in sports
_____ Big paycheck	_____ Intuitive
_____ Creative/artistic	_____ Reliable
_____ Shy	_____ Goal oriented
_____ Laid back attitude	_____ Outgoing
_____ A listener	_____ Aggressive
_____ Open minded	_____ Stable
_____ Touchy/affectionate	_____ Dependent
_____ Musical	

That was quite the list, wasn't it? No wonder it takes us forever to find the one. If you've managed to do so-Congrats!

Since you've checked off the things you value, go rate them in the order of importance to you. Thought you were done, huh? OH-This one is hard!!! (#1 is most important and so on…)

While you're thinking of preferences…your ideal perfect partner would have:

Hair color_____

Eye color_____

Body type_____

That was a tough one to go through. I know, I know…why they heck would she ask us to number them? Well, I think it's important to know what we truly value first and foremost in another.

60-How about this easy one? If you knew you were going to be stranded on an island for 1 year and you got your choice of things to bring to last you that one year, what would you decide? Now it has to be stuff in real life, no smart thinking like wishing for a boat. We're talking stranded with little provisions. Keep in mind you will be experiencing these things over and over and over and over...365 days in a row:

Food _____(better love it, cause that's all you're getting)
Junk food_____(yikes...only one?)
Music CD_____(cause yep you get to hear one over and over)
Family member/or friend _____ (but only one)
Book _____
Beverage _____
What movie _____(over and over and over)
Tool _____
One piece of sporting equipment _____
Clothing: Top _____   Bottom _____

Way better choices than what you see on those reality shows, huh? They don't give them much to start off with.

61-Speaking of which, if you were forced to be on one of the current reality shows (whether you liked it or not):

Which would it be _____

Which game show _____

62-My favorite thing to think about is if I ever won that big lottery. Some get pretty high up there in the amount, but if you won, let's say 10 million dollars, do you know what you'd do with it all? We all think about that one I'm sure, but we never really plan it all out, do we? Probably because it's a slim chance we ever win. I'm sure you'd pay off all the debts, but what about the rest? Let's see what things you have thought of. Would you?

Tell people right away   _____yes _____no

Share with family   _____yes _____no

How many friends would you help   _____yes _____no

Change your phone number _____yes _____no

Quit work right away _____yes _____no

Give to charities _____yes _____no

What would you buy? 1st :_____

2nd :_____

3rd :_____

4th :_____

5th :_____

Would you invest a big sum _____yes _____ no

Would you travel _____yes _____no

To where first _____

Who would you take _____

Would you move from where you live now _____yes _____no

Where do you see yourself living _____

Would it change who you are _____yes _____no

Would you dance on your boss's desk just for the fun of it _____yes _____no
(Oops! -I was daydreaming there for a minute!)

63-Well money isn't everything they say, although I'm sure we'd all like to verify that for ourselves, happiness is the key and you can't buy that. What are the five top things that make you happy in this life so far?

1_____

2_____

3_____

4_____

5_____

64-When was the last time you laughed so hard you darn near cried, peed your pants or your stomach hurt from it? Think back...

Were you with anyone _____ yes _____no

If yes, who _____

The occasion:

_____

_____

_____

65-Well, you've come a long way in this life so what 6 top attributes are you most proud of when you look at yourself? What internal workings do you know will always be there to see you through it all? A few of mine would be funny, stubborn, dedicated...etc.

_____   _____

_____   _____

_____   _____

We have so much to deal with in life and we question where we're heading or what's next in life, but so far so good if we're sitting looking over it all.

66-Do you believe in re-incarnation? One of those questions that you just wonder 'could it be?' If it is real, maybe my next life will be way easier. There are so many weird things to think about like have I been here before? Strange things that we just never know for sure, so let's ask a few questions on these:

Do you think reincarnation may be possible _____yes _____no

What/who do you think you might have been in previous life

_____

What would you like to come back in next life as

_____

Is there one person you know, that you feel you must've known from lifetime to lifetime

_____

Ever had a déjà vu moment _____yes _____no

Was it some place you'd never been before _____yes _____no

Was it with people you don't recall knowing _____yes _____no

Was it a conversation you suddenly predicted _____yes _____no

Were friends/family involved _____yes _____no

Describe briefly the moment you felt the déjà vu. What words set it off

_____

_____

_____

We brush those off as mere coincidences, but are they? I suppose anything is possible.

67-There are so many different, beliefs, religions, ideals and faiths. We're not going to delve into this subject much. To me, everyone believes what he or she believes and that's fine by me. But ask yourself this: If someone came along today and professed to be the higher power or God, we likely wouldn't believe (Skepticism in modern society.)

What do you think it would take for you to be convinced? It could be one or several things they'd need to do.

1 _____

2._____

3._____

4._____

5._____

68-That last question may have been difficult, but it makes us wonder. Let's delve into more things we can't see but often question. Do you believe in:

Ghosts _____yes _____no

Telepathy _____yes _____no

Miracles _____yes _____no

Haunted houses _____yes _____no

Telekinetic power _____yes _____no

The afterlife _____yes _____no

Judgment day _____yes _____no

Love at first sight _____yes _____no

Karma-Everything happens for a reason _____yes _____no

Horoscopes _____yes _____no

Card readers _____yes _____no

Psychics _____yes _____no

Mediums _____ yes _____ no

Have any odd things happened to you with any of the above? If so, when and what was it?

_____

_____

_____

69-When you walk down a street and see someone approaching from the other direction you somehow automatically know whether to smile or cross the street and avoid them. What is that I wonder?

Do you get that feeling _____yes _____no

Do you follow your signal _____yes _____no

70-Weird things we do without really thinking. It's like we're just following an internal compass. Yep, mine's been off a few times (must have been standing near a big magnet or something). I should have maybe picked better or followed instinct more. Think back over your life and all the decisions you've made, what's your ratio?

_____% Right in decisions you made.

_____% Followed first instinct

_____% Times I ignored the inner voice

71-I bet we've all had some big oops, should have moments. Mine was getting married too young. I thought I knew how it was all gonna turn out back then, but live and learn. Growing pains they call them. I keep thinking back to my childhood days when I had it all planned in my young brain. I wanted to grow up, be a veterinarian, find prince charming, have 10 kids, and horses. (Ok so not realistic at age 10).
What did you want to be when you were growing up and what things did you see in your future?

_____

_____

_____

Did you follow that dream _____yes _____no

What are you doing now

_____

_____

_____

Did you see yourself getting married _____yes_____ no

Did you find your prince charming/princess _____yes_____ no

If yes, was it on the first try _____yes _____no

Did you see yourself having kids ____yes _____no

How many did you want way back then _____

How many do you have now _____boys _____girls ____none

72-I think we all had ideas of what we'd do when we grew up. I wanted to live on a ranch surrounded by animals. The horse was my favorite and I spent many days at my friends place mucking stalls, brushing them and riding. Thinking about it now, my butt hasn't been on or near a saddle since I was 17! I have no pets, even though I grew up with them…Wow, did I miss my mark. Let's see if you got any closer.

What did you absolutely love when you were a kid and could see yourself doing or having the rest of your life?

_____

_____

_____

Do you have some of those things in your life now _____yes_____ no
If yes, what did you follow through on.

_____

_____

If no, are you still planning to have it one day _____yes _____no

What one thing are you still planning on that you can guarantee you'll get

_____

73-It's how it goes when we get busy with work, obligations and we find other things to fulfill our lives. What are the things you have now that you absolutely love in your life and can't imagine not having around? Let's go with the top 10.

_____   _____   _____

_____   _____   _____

_____   _____   _____

_____

I guess we should look back and ponder the things we thought we wanted. Turns out we probably have all we need. Life is one big adventure of experiences, twists, turns and unexpected changes. You never know what lies around that corner.

74-Keeping that in mind, we're going to do an overall view of things from where you stand right now in life, looking back at everything you've gone through up until now, how'd ya do so far?

_____Fair

_____Good

_____Great

_____Oops made a few

_____I'm still changing things

_____Perfect (don't ya want to poke these people in the eye? Perfect, I wish!)

75-In these days of fast paced life we often forget the little things. We keep busy following schedules and have so much to do, yet the small things can have the biggest impact. Let's see if you've ever experienced some of the following:

Random act of kindness by perfect stranger towards you _____yes _____no
What was it

_____

_____

_____

Have you ever done one for a stranger _____yes _____no

What was it

_____

_____

_____

Thinking back, what was the nicest thing you've ever done for a friend or family member?

_____

_____

What was the nicest thing family or a friend did for you?

_____

_____

76-Since you're looking back, if you could have known back then what you know now, (hindsight), would you have pursued a different path? Is there one thing you have a gift for that you only realize now? This is the first book I've written and at age 44. Perhaps I should have taken the time back then to learn more about writing. Is there anything you wished you would have tried?

_____Yes or _____ No

If yes, I should have

_____

_____

_____

77-Astrology, now there's a subject! Horoscopes, card reading, tea leaf reading-some believe and some don't. The mystical wisdom of what was meant to be. Some simply read their horoscope, while others try to live by it and others don't even bother to think about the cosmic meaning of everything. Let's ask a few questions:

What sign are you? _____

Have you read what the cosmos say your traits are supposed to be? If you have, the top 6 words that describe your sign are:

_____   _____

_____   _____

_____...._____

Do you think you have these traits _____ yes _____no ____some

Do you read your horoscope

_____Daily   _____Once in a while   _____Never read it

Do you get readings done professionally ____yes _____no

Do you believe in it all _____yes ____no ____kind of

Would you like to get a reading _____yes _____no _____kind of

78-Did you know there is a Chinese calendar which shows you are born in a certain animal year. For example, I am born in 1964 'the year of the Dragon'. What symbol are you?

_____

(you might have to research this one)

79-If it's all true, there would be signs we just don't get along with naturally and some we always get along with well. We all know people born under different signs. Looking at your friends and family, is there one sign you more often than not have a hard time really getting along with?

Sign: _____

What traits don't you like about that sign

_____

What sign are most of your friends that you get along with

_____

What are their best traits

_____   _____   _____   _____

Your male best friends is a _____

Your female best friend is a _____

Your partner/spouse is a _____

Your children's signs are (blended families included)

_____   _____   _____   _____   _____

_____   _____   _____   _____   _____

80-We all have heartfelt moments. At times we sit and think about everyone that touched our soul. We can forget to say the things we should and in some situations, wish we would have said something. There isn't enough time in a day, we get busy and put it off until tomorrow. Rarely do we follow through, life keeps us in our routine or we're afraid of putting ourselves out there. Here are some things to think about.

How do you normally show affection to friends

_____

And to Family

_____

Do you to tell people how you feel about them _____yes _____no

Do you try to show them in your own way _____yes _____no

Do you end a conversation with 'love you' _____yes _____no

Do you hug your friends and family: _____Once in a while

_____Every time I see them

_____On special occasions only

_____Never done it but want to

_____Don't do that stuff

Have you ever sat and told them what they really mean to you

_____yes _____no _____some I have

Do you wish you had that opportunity _____yes _____no.

If yes, more so with: family_____ or friends _____

How many people would you like to say something to _____

Do you just hope they know it _____yes_____ no

Will you try to be more open _____yes _____no

81-Well that's a hard question, so let's put the shoe on the other foot and ask how you feel about others expressing themselves to you. Some people are open to hearing things and some aren't.

Do you like hearing how a person honestly feels about you _____yes _____no

Do you like getting hugs and affection _____yes _____no

Is there anyone in particular you wish you could find out how they feel about you

_____yes _____ no   If yes, who: _____

If you could ask that person one question about what they think about you, what would your question be?

_____

82-Some people just weren't raised with expressing affection, it was more of a silent fact and you just knew what they thought or how they felt, while some were raised in overly expressive households. For my family, it was always done with humor.

What environment did you experience?

_____Always open and affectionate

_____Rarely open and affectionate

_____We knew where we all stood

_____Expressed it on occasion

_____We didn't talk about things at that level

_____Don't ask

_____We did it with laughter

_____Surrounded by love

Are you following in the same footsteps? Sometimes we follow the same patterns and at others, we do the total opposite. It depends who we take after I suppose.

83-You can even have two complete opposite styles in one set of parents. Genetics…yikes! So think of both sides, let's see who you figure you're more like.

In looks you take after which side the most   _____mom _____dad

In personality you take after your   _____mom _____dad

In humor it's more like your   _____mom _____dad

In intelligence it's more like   _____mom _____dad

In attitude it's more like   _____mom _____dad

In emotional things I'm more like   _____mom _____dad

In body structure I'm more like   _____mom _____dad

In stubbornness I'm more like   _____mom _____dad

I get my love of :_____from _____mom _____dad
     (hobby or skill)

Talented just like my   _____mom _____dad

I show affection like my   _____mom _____dad

Well how'd ya do, which side is stronger?
       Totals= _____ _____

84- We're darn proud of some of those things. It makes us who we are. But ya know… there is always that one quirk we wish we didn't take after so much. Whether the big ears from Mom's side or the dry humor from Dad's…

Which one physical thing do you wish you didn't have?

_____

What one character trait do you wish you didn't have?

_____

85-It's good to know where we came from, it may help us know where we're going. Speaking of which, do you find that you are doing stuff your parents used to do? Remember when you were young and they did something and you'd say-"when I grow up, I'm never going to do that!"…then suddenly you're doing it?

For me, it was Mom always having that tissue ready for spillage. She'd lick it then clean off my face. (Eww, I used to hate that!) A few years back I did the exact same thing-Yikes!

What things do you find you're repeating (may be a few here)

_____

_____

_____

86-Yep, things change with time. Think of all the things you used to love as a child, teen or young adult. When loud music was great and now quiet is good. I used to say "you know you're getting old when it's too loud."(guess I'm getting there) So let's list the things that just kinda happened. Check it off if you can relate:

_____Sleeping in: What's that? Even on your day off you're up early

_____You seem to always be busy, you find things to do

_____Music is ok once in awhile

_____Loud music for too long gives you headaches

_____You suddenly wear dress clothes more than jeans

_____Sandals and socks

_____Let the answering machine pick up (we used to race to the phone didn't we?)

_____Plan projects that we don't really need

_____Asleep early most nights-even on weekends

_____A night out ends at 1 A.M., not like the good old days watching the sun come up!

_____Don't want to do anything that may look silly (remember when we didn't care?)

_____Looking at the world with skepticism instead of innocence

_____The spit on the tissue and wiping someone else's mouth

_____Carrying a hankie

_____Wearing an undershirt under a dress shirt

_____Rock music isn't your thing anymore

_____Starting to wear more polyester

Add some of your own please:

_____

_____

_____

87-I looked forward to growing up. I couldn't wait to get my own place, get a job and make money. I could do what I want, when I wanted. (Uh huh, what was I thinking?) Now, I put this question here because we all complain about something, so let's get it off your chest. Which things bother you about being grown up? On a scale from 1-10, 1 being that it's the most aggravating and 10 being it's no big deal--rate each line accordingly.

_____Utilities we pay every month (wow, I use how much water?)

_____Demands of work and the boss (so much for doing what I want, when I want)

_____Taxes we pay (doesn't pay to get a raise sometimes)

_____Politics in workplaces (man, can't we all just get along)

_____You want how much to fix the vehicle? (Surprise!)

_____Amount of school supplies kids need (are we stocking the schools?)

_____Cost of housing (is it me, doesn't seem in line with wages does it?)

_____Health care costs, doctors, dentists, medicine (Wow-Best never get sick)

_____Cost of vehicles now- (it's like 1/3 of house values)

_____The more guarded everyone seems about opening up

_____Yard work! I just cut the darn grass and pulled weeds

_____Cost of maintenance and fixing stuff around the home

Go ahead, add your own and vent it all out:

_____

_____

88-Onto brighter things-inventions! The things people create to make our lives easier. They make a ton of money doing it: Gadgets for the kitchen, robot vacuums, handy tools…all those little things that are a flash in the pan. Some worked and some we now see at every flea market and garage sale. Items you see on those late night TV shopping channels. So let's ask:

Did you buy one _____yes _____no _____it was a gift

What was it _____

Did it work _____

Did it do all it was supposed to _____yes ____ no and for how long? _____

Did you like it _____

Where is it now _____

Stupidest one you ever saw was a _____

Best one you ever saw was a _____

Bet if you go through your cupboards and garage, you just might find a few in there.

89-Gadgets, do-hickeys, whatcha-macallits…all things to enhance our life, with all the options I just don't know what to buy anymore. The simple vacuum is now available as upright, canister, hepa, wind tunnel etc… you get lost in the knowing what's good anymore! The same goes for most things we buy, so are you:

_____An informed shopper, (check all the latest data)

_____I stick with what I know (I use what I use because I always used it)

_____Risk taker (I'll try anything)

_____Trendy shopper (I want the most current styles)

_____Bargain shopper (I get what is cheapest)

_____Investment shopper (I'll spend more for a better warranty)

90- Ever look at the electronics today? It's crazy all we can have in our own home. It seems wonderful until you get it home and realize you have to set it all up. (Some assembly required). Yikes! Now for me, I read the manual, map it out, set the parts out and then phone a friend. I suck at connecting wires! Let's see how you handle things:

_____You wing it (try to figure it all out on your own-if there's extra parts you'll deal with em later)

_____Step by step (you follow along with the manual as best you can)

_____Studious type (you read every manual front to back then start)

_____Yikes!! (ask someone to set it all up for you)

_____Hire help (pay store personnel to come do it all)

_____Magic person (you just know how to do it all so no problem-you're the one people call)

Who is it you call on the most in those times_____

91-With tackling stuff we learn so many things along the way. We've all done things that we're darn proud of, whether it's something we built, repaired...etc. That moment where you just felt proud that you did it all by yourself! It could be you finished a basement, built a deck, out lasted someone in a competition, created an art piece... so what are the Woo Hoo! I did it moments?
Must have a few in this life...list the top 10:

_____   _____

_____   _____

_____   _____

_____   _____

_____   _____

92-Some things we even had help with, when friends and family pitched in to lend a hand. Many moments of shared time with working together (Kinda a warm moment) I am truly blessed by the amount of help I get sometimes. It's funny how you get busy and never really think of those memories regularly.

So list the top 10 people who throughout your lifetime have been there for you in those moments:

_____   _____

_____   _____

_____   _____

_____   _____

_____   _____

93-If you could get in touch with any one person from your past, either a friend from long ago or a family member, maybe an old flame...whoever it was that you lost touch with. Maybe it was a disagreement or life just moved forward and they slipped away:

Who would it be _____

They were your _____

Why _____

_____

What would be the first thing you say to them

_____

Ever try to track them down? _____yes _____no

94-Thinking along those same lines, we all wish we were understood a bit more by someone. People sometimes don't see eye to eye. Families disagree, friends have rifts and lovers quarrel. At times we never finish what should've been said. If you could sit down with any one person in your life now and have that heart to heart with them and they'd tell you the truth and nothing but the truth...

Who would that be _____

Why

_____

_____

Now the flip-side: Who do you think would want to sit down with you and you had to tell the whole truth and nothing but the truth:

Who would that be _____
Why?

_____

_____

95-It seems life is difficult at times, but I think that's how it's supposed to be. I wonder if we all had read more books on psychology growing up, would we have figured out more of these things along the way. If you could take one and only one lesson in life that you know now, back to when you were young, what would you tell yourself?

If I knew then, what I know now…I would tell myself to:

_____

_____

96-It's always easier looking back, isn't it? Now looking into the future with all the lessons learned up until now, what one lesson do you think you need to practice more to make life better for you from here on in?

_____

_____

97-Wow, we're coming close to being done all this thinking. If you could give this book to any one person in your life and they answered all the questions, who would you want to see the answers from the most?

Who _____

Now if you could give this to a famous person and got to read all their answers

Who _____

98-Hasn't it been nice to spend time with yourself? To think about things long forgotten- friends, hopes, dreams and firsts. I picked your brain and you're probably ready to throw this book out the window. (Who asks these kinda questions anyhow?)

Maybe if we all stopped to understand one another a little more, life would be a little easier or happier. Well if not happier, we'd gain an understanding of each other. We could reach across distances that somehow grew in our lives.

So how do you feel about others knowing about how you think and who you are?

Will you leave this out for anyone to read (new coffee table item) _____yes _____no

Will you ask your friends do one and share answers ____yes ____no

Will you ask your family do one and share answers ____yes ____no

Will you keep this as a keepsake and revisit it in future ____yes ____no

99-Your life is all it is supposed to be. Heck, it got you this far, didn't it? So looking ahead what do you see in the next 10 years of your life?

Any big purchase ahead, if so, what top two things do you plan on getting in the next year

_____

_____

Planned a get-away vacation, if so where

_____

_____

Re-visiting of old friends

_____

_____

Anything you want to change?

_____

_____

Any new things you want to try?

_____

_____

Anything exciting planned?

_____

_____

100-You are you and life wasn't always easy or fair for that matter. You've learned to get through things to this point, having some good, some bad and some just okay moments. Everything in life has brought you to this point.

If you could make one promise to yourself to better your life in some way…perhaps to take up a hobby or reach out more…who knows, maybe you'll want to listen to others thoughts or go do something fun. Finish those projects you started. There are so many things we put off to the wayside that are important so let's make a change for you, today. This one is all about you, Sunshine. Fill in the blank, I promise I will:

_____

_____

_____

I'm hoping you enjoyed the time you've spent thinking about life and what it means to you. Where you've been and what you've learned is important. I plan to continue these books as my way of making the world stop for a moment and just appreciate who we are. It's my hope that this helps family and friends share thoughts and experiences. Seems in this world of fast paced life we often don't get the chance to make time for one another.

Wendy Proteau

Blessed with three siblings and parents who supported my hopes, I was raised in a small Canadian town, in an average middle-class family. Single at age forty-something, I'm still figuring life out daily. Being a combination of realist and dreamer, you can only imagine the confusion that goes on internally. Half of me writes a story with 'the happily ever after', the other half, edits the work and keeps it more realistic.

I'd never written more than a grocery list until 2009. It came out of nowhere as I sat at my computer following an idea. The '*Sit N Do Nothing Hamster Series*' is my way to bring us all a little closer in this technological world. The workbooks of self-discovery are a way to share tidbits of who we are, in the here and now. Each of the seven volumes, designed for a specific audience, asks the reader about their lives. I have many more ideas to expand the series. This hamster never quits! They are now available via print on demand.

Finding my inner voice, I decided to try my hand at a fiction. *'And When'* was written from September 2010–January 2011. Receiving many reviews, the story resonated, often bringing them to tears, laughter, and at times… needing a cold towel.

Taking months to edit the final draft, I began to miss that creative energy and *'Now What'* the sequel was started in 2012 and published in 2013. The story continues to place difficult hurdles, forcing the characters to veer from their chosen paths.

My life would be nothing without the people who have touched my soul. Friends, family, co-workers, relatives…have all been there through the good and bad. Everything takes hard work and nothing ever comes easy. Well at least not in my life. I firmly believe that karma plays an important role. It brings us the people we are meant to meet, challenges we have to overcome, lessons we need to learn and dreams we are meant to reach for.

The Sit 'N' Do Nothing Hamster Series
Continues with:

Unlock Your Hamster-Volume One
An introduction to the series

The Single Man Hamster-Volume Two

The Single Woman Hamster-Volume Three

Hamsters Unite-The Relationship-Volume Four
Dating, Married or Living Together

Heart Broke Hamster-Volume Five
For the tough spots of break-up, divorce or loss

The Gotta Have Hamster-Volume Six
Advertising and what you buy into

The Hospital Hamster-Volume Seven
For those in hospital or home recuperating

www.wendiann.com

www.ingramcontent.com/pod-product-compliance
Lightning Source LLC
Chambersburg PA
CBHW080528030426

42337CB00023B/4665